The Taxidermist
Shazea Quraishi

VERVE
POETRY PRESS
BIRMINGHAM

PUBLISHED BY VERVE POETRY PRESS
https://vervepoetrypress.com
mail@vervepoetrypress.com

All rights reserved
© 2020 Shazea Quraishi

The right of Shazea Quraishi to be identified as author of this work has been asserted in accordance with section 77 of the Copyright, Designs and Patents Act 1988.

No part of this work may be reproduced, stored or transmitted in any form or by any means, graphic, electronic, recorded or mechanical, without the prior written permission of the publisher.

FIRST PUBLISHED OCT 2020

Printed and bound in the UK
by Positive Print, Birmingham

ISBN: 978-1-912565-44-3

Oh you out there – run, it is day, run everywhere –
rise fall sink breathe – open up – happen.

Jorie Graham, Vigil

The Taxidermist

Day 1

She wakes to birdsong   sun slats on the floor
suitcase by the door spills clothes   quiet
of the house a cocoon   a skin
At the table she waits for the mouse to thaw
    scalpel tweezers calipers
    pins pipecleaners wire scissors
    needle thread straw
Begins
taking apart
putting together

Day 2

Working
light changes   the day stretching like a cat   jumps
into evening

The washing machine on   sound of it company   a blanket
round her   she falls asleep on the sofa
   wakes to dark
Outside hums with life   bare feet in grass
all around   night sky   stars   ~~crickets~~ grasshoppers   a dog
barks   answering barks across the valley
Inside a moth flutters against the window
mistaking lamplight for the moon
Soon there are more moths more insects tapping the glass
She turns off the lamp   sits in the dark

No more. Good.

she → I

a white mouse, a feeder mouse

soft drift of white
his modest truth disarms me

forehead
ears   feet
        mouth
        a dim rose
        with teeth

I admire
this raw meat of us
this ease

        dream of radishes, wheat

Day 3

Sunrise
the highest tree in the garden is the first to be lit
Birds come   one orange-red bellied   another bright-yellow black-headed   black wings tipped with white
and another   a pair
Sky blue as the bucket by the tap
air cool   an ant crosses her foot
   bees in the lavender bush

A bird perches in a leafless tree
dun-coloured   long-tailed   quiet
watches her watching
preens under its wings

Here   the other side of the world
grass looks different
earth bleached by sun   flowers blaze
air smells   how to describe it   orange

a white mouse (2)

hiatus
time teems
                              thaws

she ate
she saw

   oh muse   most
   whose tame wish
   was oats

(how I adore this somewhat wise housemate)

Her hands intent precise thinking
miracle how living works stops
careful labour to preserve restore what? ~~limbo?~~
past-in-present perhaps an imprint a 3-dimensional holding
~~of memory~~ of once-being

She once heard someone say this is craft it lacks edge
   (advantage power urgency force)
gets up to shift thoughts

White heat dust rises from the dirt road dogs barking follow
her to the first shop avocado mango beans tomato lime
   words rusty in her mouth

a white mouse (3)

what has a white mouse to show us?

I meet him
white mute item
    (fate
      air hums with it)

he was
he is

I sew him shut
wish him home

She remembers
swimming in a river by her brother's house
its current cold   insistent
how once she let it carry her too far before climbing the high
bank to walk back over pine needles   hard earth   stones
how her brother later told her he watched from a window
until he saw her
red swimsuit flickering through the trees

Day 6

Morning light   coffee
white butterfly on the coral bougainvillea
   The average lifespan of a butterfly is a month   this small
   butterfly will live perhaps a week   that's a full life

Hummingbird?
perhaps the idea of the bird
rather than the bird itself
  something
      speed and stop
          says hummingbird
Yesika   the woman at the shop   said if you wait for it
or want it too much   it won't come
   How to not want something?

        Van playing a jingle about propane gas supply goes by
        dust settles back on the road

She takes the hummingbird from the freezer
The boy down the road found it under a hibiscus bush
they like red flowers   *Chuparrosa* he called it
Rose-drinker
    Sometimes they sleep so deeply   *letargo*
    it's like they're dead   But this is not sleep   he said
    I checked

Nestled in the palm of her hand   wings tucked in as though
cold   she regrets her wish to see one so close

Rose Drinker

rise
keen siren
      reside in rosier din

seek red
drink

Day

The boy   his name is Havi   returns with 4 hummingbirds
pitiful things   poorly preserved   bought from a man in the city
   They make powerful love-charms   he says   the bird with a
   keepsake from the beloved   covered with honey in a jar
   sealed with a spell

She tries to explain   only animals who died a natural or
unpreventable death   sees his face
   thank you   she says quickly
   and   sadness has its own beauty

He is wearing the same blue t-shirt   freshly laundered
shy looks towards the animals on the shelf
She shows him the mouse curled up
inside a pale green china cup   fur so soft
   For you

When he is gone she examines the birds
one is smaller than any she's seen
    impossible wonder magic of it
    head the size of her fingernail
In her palm it weighs perhaps a penny
irridescent throat feathers electric pink purple
fat little body
Rot is beginning   nothing can be done except learn its name
   Bumblebee Hummingbird (Atthis heloisa)
learn that it lives in the Sierra Gorda   far from here
   despair pity anger in her throat   she makes a small pyre
outside the back door
kindling and dried flowers on a bed of stones
acrid smoke as it burns

Later she will lay the 3 remaining birds
side by side
on a bed of straw
in a box painted with red flowers

Day

Time has expanded or shrunk   the days merging

Word spreads
her freezer begins to fill

Each morning she watches the sun rise behind the hills
light bringing birds to the garden
watches their here-there flit
how they are rarely alone

She is working on a hummingbird   Havi watches   surprising
how little he disturbs
   Why?
   Some animals haven't had the chance to live their lives fully
   feeder mice are bred as food for snakes and lizards
   Death is a peaceful state   I want them to look as if they're
   sleeping   as if they might wake up

   Except for birds   my wish for them is flight

Later she calls him to look closer   calls him by her brother's
name   Is it his concentration his quiet thinking look or
memory of her brother small as this

Havi says on YouTube at his cousin's house there is a man who
hunts big animals
has them stuffed and put on his wall
   Don't you get sad?
   Yes   but   these are not trophies   I want
She grasps   makes a gesture of prayer   of thanks
   to honour to serve as witness to their lives
She wants to say   life is often so brief so unbearably
precious
   Also I hate waste

Hummingbird (colibrí)

humble icon
    gold blurring
    indigo idling

no climbing   no chirr
numb
    blind
        rigid

cold rumour in limbo

    It's not fair   time is not enough
    for hummingbirds   or grandmothers
    sometimes baby sisters   his face serious

Before he goes he takes from his pocket a pale pink stone
    for you
Later turning it over   she will see he has drawn a smiley face

Dusky Hummingbird

dun bird
unbusy ruby nib
iris inky

sky hung hymn

Rufous Hummingbird

sun god in ruins
no song   no humming
rush dimming
burnish subduing

hours shroud in bruising indigo

Reading

   a devastating pestilence swept through London   the dying boarded up in their homes   theatres bear-baiting yards brothels closed   As Shakespeare wrote a Greenland shark still alive today swam untroubled through the waters of the northern seas   For thousands of years Greenland sharks have swum in silence   above them the world has burned rebuilt burned
   the largest, a 16-foot female   between 272 and 512 years old   size a relatively good indicator of age   there are records of sharks reaching 24 feet long   it's very possible there are sharks in the water today well into their sixth century
   not obviously beautiful   its face is blunt its fins stunted   smell of pee   In Inuit legend the shark is said to have arisen from the chamberpot of Sedna goddess of the sea   At full speed with strenuous effort it moves between 1.7 and 2.2 mph
   They lead secret lives   prefer to be close to the bottom of the ocean   where it's dark and cold   six Eiffel Towers deep   Nobody has seen one give birth   they live so far below ships and divers   we do not know   they may be everywhere   the ocean goes deep and cold   they could be closer than we think

Allen's Hummingbird

small sabred dream

hunger banished
midair blur and rush
           begun
           ended

remain here in mild slumber

darling bud
un burden

Scott's Oriole

    rise   rosiest soloist
                           stir

    cross isles
    crest cities

    resist soil's cloister

Day 17

Someone brings her   what is it?
a Mexican mouse opossum
ugly (not often she thinks this)   is it the pointy shrewish snout
dark bulging eyes long fingers toes bulbous tips
    what to do with this?

That night she dreams she is fluid
moving through water   light ripple glimmers
across the blue tiled floor   she surfaces
    Huitzilopochtli the hummingbird god appears
    floating in the air   speaks
    words like wind through a door

Mexican mouse opossum

supine campesino
no nip no pounce no noise
                       suspense

someone's cousin
                       compassion comes

I coax ~~escape?~~ ~~séance?~~
    a sepia pause
    immense comma

Day

Havi brings a pillowcase   it's heavy   grinning he
spills out 2 enormous snakes   his uncle found them
under the house   near the baby's room

She has never seen snakes this big this close   terrifying
beautiful intricate markings
The snakes are longer than her arm   almost as thick
    Look   he opens the mouth   at the fangs

She reads
Coatl is the Nahuatl word for serpent
that Aztec gods include *Quetzalcoatl* (feathered serpent)
Mixcoatl (Cloud Serpent) *Xiuhcoatl* (Fire Serpent) and
(She of the Serpent Skirt) *Coatlicue* mother of *Huitzilopochtli*
that the habit of snakes to shed their skin each year symbolizes
renewal   transformation
that their ability to move freely between water   earth   and the
forest canopy   makes them intermediaries

Remembering the Aztec double-headed serpent she once saw
at the British Museum   she reads that
double-headed animals represent the sky   the open mouth
a gateway to the underworld

2 Olmecan pit vipers

2 serpents
cleave
rise
no more to coil
or creep in soil
eternal veil in place   remain
          rapt in aconite   copper   stone
          not victor   vermin   victim
nor monster   no sin
ripple venom nerve
opaline silence a
revelation
omen
lament

Day 20

Morning
light spills into day

    Am I trying to cheat death?   No
    dead is dead   no longer here   but
    something remains   stronger than memory

        I was
        you are

The tree across the road buzzes
    hummingbirds or bees?
She closes the gate behind her.

NOTES

The taxidermy poems employ an anagram form inspired by the French post-surrealist group OULIPO (Ouvroir de Littérature Potentielle), a gathering of mathmeticians, scientists and writers who embrace constraint as a means of triggering ideas and inspiration.

'Reading' cites text from 'Consider the Greenland Shark' by Katherine Rundell in *The London Review of Books*, 7 May 2020

ABOUT THE AUTHOR

Shazea Quraishi is a Pakistani-born Canadian poet and translator based in London. An alumni of The Complete Works I, her first pamphlet, *The Courtesans Reply*, was published by Flipped Eye in 2012 and *The Art of Scratching*, her first book-length collection, was published by Bloodaxe Books in 2015.

Her poems have appeared in UK and US publications including *The Guardian, The Financial Times, Poetry Review* and most recently *The Hudson Review & New England Review*.

ACKNOWLEDGEMENTS

Grateful acknowledgements to *The Hudson Review: the British issue, Spring 2020* where versions of the white mouse poems appeared. Thanks also to Stuart Bartholomew for his kindness and support.

The work and ideas of taxidermy artists Divya Anantharaman, Mickey Alice Kwapis and Polly Morgan were a key source of inspiration, as was Mary Jo Bang's poem 'You Were You Are Elegy'.

ABOUT VERVE POETRY PRESS

Verve Poetry Press is a quite new and already award-winning press that focussed initially on meeting a local need in Birmingham - a need for the vibrant poetry scene here in Brum to find a way to present itself to the poetry world via publication. Co-founded by Stuart Bartholomew and Amerah Saleh, it now publishes poets from all corners of the UK - poets that speak to the city's varied and energetic qualities and will contribute to its many poetic stories.

Added to this is a colourful pamphlet series, many featuring poets who have performed at our sister festival - and a poetry show series which captures the magic of longer poetry performance pieces by festival alumni such as Polarbear, Matt Abbott and Geraldine Carver.

Like the festival, we strive to think about poetry in inclusive ways and embrace the multiplicity of approaches towards this glorious art.

In 2019 the press was voted Most Innovative Publisher at the Saboteur Awards, and won the Publisher's Award for Poetry Pamphlets at the Michael Marks Awards.

www.vervepoetrypress.com
@VervePoetryPres
mail@vervepoetrypress.com